Haatchi *and* Little B

www.**randomhousechildrens**.co.uk

Haatchi
and
Little B

Two best friends.
One very special true story.

Junior Edition

WENDY HOLDEN

RED FOX

HAATCHI & LITTLE B – JUNIOR EDITION
A RED FOX BOOK 978 1 782 95468 2
First published in Great Britain by Bantam Press,
an imprint of Transworld Publishers
A Penguin Random House Company

Penguin
Random House
UK

Abridged junior edition published by Red Fox,
an imprint of Random House Children's Publishers UK
Transworld edition published 2014

This Red Fox edition published 2015

1 3 5 7 9 10 8 6 4 2

Copyright © Owen Howkins and Wendy Holden, 2014

The Random House Group Limited supports the Forest Stewardship Council® (FSC®),
the leading international forest-certification organisation. Our books carrying the FSC
label are printed on FSC®-certified paper. FSC is the only forest-certification scheme
supported by the leading environmental organisations, including Greenpeace. Our paper
procurement policy can be found at www.randomhouse.co.uk/environment

MIX
Paper from
responsible sources
FSC® C016897
FSC
www.fsc.org

Set in Bembo

Red Fox Books are published by Random House Children's Publishers UK,
61–63 Uxbridge Road, London W5 5SA

www.randomhousechildrens.co.uk
www.totallyrandombooks.co.uk
www.randomhouse.co.uk

Addresses for companies within The Random House Group Limited can be found at:
www.randomhouse.co.uk/offices.htm

THE RANDOM HOUSE GROUP Limited Reg. No. 954009

A CIP catalogue record for this book is available from the British Library.

Printed and bound by CPI Group (UK) Ltd, Croydon, CR0 4YY.

*This book is dedicated to those who are different
and to the humans and animals who love them
all the more because of it*

PROLOGUE

Lifting his head, he sniffed the chill night air with his wet black nose. He tried to move but it hurt too much, so he slumped back down where he lay. Peering right and left through amber eyes, he wondered where his human had gone and why he'd been abandoned there in the dark. Had he done something wrong? Would someone come to help him?

The Miracle Dog

Nobody knows for certain how the five-month-old Anatolian Shepherd dog who was later given the name 'Stray: E10' came to be on the railway tracks that cold night of 9 January 2012. But that night two miracles happened.

The first miracle is that as a train headed towards him, the dog managed to flatten himself against the track-bed. Sadly, he was unable to escape the train altogether and its wheels almost cut off his back

3

left leg, but he did manage to keep himself alive.

The second miracle is that this amazing dog somehow managed to lift his body onto his three uninjured legs and limp away to what he hoped was a place of safety.

For a while the abandoned dog lay there in the cold – without food or water, hurt, and sniffing at and occasionally licking his wounds.

Then he was spotted by a train driver, who called his manager, Nigel Morris, and asked him to investigate.

Nigel did just that.

Carrying a torch and letting himself into the secure area via a locked metal gate, Nigel began searching for the dog he had been told was on the railway line. The area where it had been sighted was very busy that night, with a total of four railway lines carrying passengers to London's Stansted Airport and to Cambridge, as well as freight trains to and from the goods yard.

Nigel searched along the track with his torch until eventually he spotted a shadow between the rails.

It was a dog! A dog, just lying there flat on its tummy without moving.

Nigel approached cautiously, and when he got closer he saw, to his surprise, that the animal was still alive, though its left rear leg and paw were covered in blood.

Nigel quickly realized that the dog was too severely injured to attack him so he tried to shift it off the rails, but the dog was a big one, and it was clear he wouldn't be able to manage on his own. He called his control room and asked them to contact the animal-rescue charity, the RSPCA, and get them to send someone to help him. Then he stayed near the injured dog and waited.

Siobhan Trinnaman was the RSPCA's uniformed welfare officer on duty that winter's night. She received a call just after 7 p.m. to attend a 'dog on the line'. She moved quickly: she jumped into her van with the RSPCA logo on the side and drove to the area, which was very close to the site of the Olympic Park.

Nigel met her on the street and then led her to the edge of the busy line that transported people and produce across the country and beyond.

As trains continued to trundle past, Siobhan picked her way over the uneven pebbly ground to where Nigel had discovered the dog. Shining the beam of her torch left and right, she eventually found the animal lying between the tracks. She could see immediately that it was seriously hurt. Standing a safe distance from where it lay, Siobhan played her torchlight along its body and noted that it was a male dog with serious injuries to the lower limbs. But she was relieved. The dog lifted his head and looked straight at her.

Then she heard something that made her gasp. Jumping back against a fence, she realized that another train was approaching.

Nigel quickly reassured her. 'It's OK,' he said. 'Watch. The dog knows what to do. The trains just ride over it. There's just enough room as long as it doesn't try to get up.'

The two grown-ups pressed back and held their

breath as a huge train rattled towards the dog. Siobhan watched in amazement as the animal, ears flattened to his head, simply lay back down and let the train rumble right over the top of him. As soon as the final carriage had passed, he lifted his head again – ears pricked – and looked across at them, as if to reassure himself that they were still there.

The minute she saw the pleading look in the dog's eyes, Siobhan begged Nigel to get the railway line shut down as quickly as possible.

Nigel immediately radioed his control room and had the line temporarily closed so that he and Siobhan could cross safely to where the injured dog lay. As soon as they were promised that all trains had been stopped in both directions further up the line, they hurried to his side.

The first thing Siobhan noticed was that the top of the dog's head was swollen. His leg and tail were badly mangled too, and his tail especially was losing blood. She couldn't tell if he had any internal injuries but he didn't appear to be too tender when she examined him.

A lot of animals as badly hurt as he was would have growled if she even came close, and almost certainly tried to bite her; she carried a muzzle just in case. But this gentle giant didn't seem to mind her touching him at all, and only whimpered a little when she did so.

With some difficulty, she and Nigel took one end of the dog each and managed to get him up onto three legs before carrying him 200 metres to where she'd parked her van. Apart from the odd whimper, he barely made a sound as they moved him and then lifted him into the back. Siobhan settled him onto bedding on his uninjured side and thanked Nigel for his help.

Nigel watched as Siobhan's van sped away. For a moment he thought about trying to adopt the dog, but he knew that with his working hours, it wasn't possible. He really hoped the poor creature would be OK . . .

2

Stray: E10

Siobhan drove as quickly as she could to the RSPCA's Harmsworth Memorial Animal Hospital in Holloway, North London. The hospital treats more than nine thousand animals every year – including many stray and injured dogs.

The young dog who'd been found on the railway tracks cried out a couple of times during the twenty-five-minute journey to the hospital, especially when his tail or leg touched the side of the van, but apart from that he was surprisingly calm and quiet.

When Siobhan eventually arrived, her clothes covered in the dog's blood, she was assisted by two of the vet nurses, who helped her lift him onto a trolley and wheeled him inside.

She recorded the dog as 'Stray: E10', as E10 was the start of the postcode where he had been discovered, and then she left him in the care of the hospital.

Siobhan never forgot him. 'He really stuck in my mind, and not just because of where and how he was found,' she remembered later. 'There was a look in his eyes that made me think about him long afterwards.'

A lot of different people from all walks of life would go on to say the same thing about this very special creature.

Stan McCaskie was the senior vet on duty at the hospital that night. He examined the dog's wounds and did all he could to stop the bleeding.

'I'll never forget seeing this big dog being wheeled towards me on the trolley, half sitting up and looking all around him,' Stan said. 'When I was told he'd been hit by a train I couldn't believe it.'

Stan knew that the important thing was to stabilize the dog after the shock of his experience. He placed him on a drip that would get fluid inside him and rehydrate him, and he gave him some painkillers and antibiotics, and then cleaned and dressed his wounds. His tail was almost completely missing, but Stan was most worried about his back leg.

The staff laid the dog on a duvet in a large, warm, quiet kennel and the vet nurses on duty were asked to check on him throughout the night.

It was so sad to see a beautiful young animal like this in such a terrible state and 'Stray: E10' won the hearts of everyone who saw him. Although he was so poorly, he still looked up hopefully every time anyone came near.

The injured dog survived his first night at the hospital, and then the next, and those caring for him began to feel more hopeful.

Still no owner came forward to claim him or to report a dog of his description missing; nor was he microchipped, which was unusual for such an expensive and relatively rare breed of dog.

Once the shock had worn off, the dog was in a lot of pain from his injuries and as soon as he was well enough, he had a serious operation.

While he was asleep, his tail was removed almost to the base of the spine and his injured back leg removed close to the hip.

Over the next few days the RSPCA discussed what they were going to do with their patient. Although he was such a kind and gentle dog, they knew he was going to grow into a massive animal and they wondered how he would cope with only three legs.

The hospital staff then just had to hope that the right home could be found for him.

A New Name and
a New Home

No one knew the big dog's name, but one by one the
Harmsworth staff fell for the animal, who looked
a bit like a cuddly bear. Their new patient constantly
craved human affection. As before, almost as soon
as he came round from his operation he tried to get
up to greet anyone who approached him.

The staff soon agreed that the forgiving Anatolian
Shepherd needed a proper name, not just a postcode.

Someone came up with the name 'Haatchi'. It came from the name of a pure-bred Japanese Akita dog called Hachikō who lived in the 1920s. He was so devoted to his master that he waited every night at the train station for him to return home from work.

Everyone agreed that this was the perfect name for Stray: E10. The name stuck, and that was that!

Even though he now had a name, Haatchi still had a long way to go. If he made it, he'd face a lot of expensive health problems that would make it even harder to find him the right home. Any dog that has lost a leg needs time and space to get used to his new shape and work out how to move again. As he tried to get used to having only three legs, Haatchi lost his balance and fell over a lot – especially on uneven or slippery surfaces.

Haatchi was eager to move out of his cage: the small space was obviously making him feel stressed, and he was whining constantly.

Haatchi had arrived at Harmsworth as little

more than a confused puppy, but in a matter of weeks he'd been forced to grow up very fast. He'd been through the worst experience of his life but had somehow emerged from it stronger, and now he was ready for a temporary foster home until he could be found somewhere permanent.

Anatolian Shepherds, which are in part descended from Mastiffs, are also known as Turkish Shepherd Guard Dogs because they are good at protecting large flocks of sheep in their original home of the Anatolian region of Turkey.

They may start off as cute, fluffy puppies but they grow quickly and need to mix from an early age with other dogs and humans. As with all large breeds of dog, they need a lot of space, plenty of exercise, and a good trainer so they don't become too powerful to handle.

The hospital managed to find Lorraine Coyle, a dog-walker and minder, as a foster mum for Haatchi for a little while. She had successfully fostered many times before, but she quickly realized that Haatchi wasn't a normal case.

Lorraine had been told that the animal who needed her help had been abandoned by a railway track and that he was still recovering from a huge operation. Her heart went out to him. 'That poor dog must have had a terrible time,' she said. 'Life was entirely different to how he remembered it.' And she was happy to take Haatchi in until he could be found a proper home.

So the handover was arranged and Haatchi arrived at her house.

Although Haatchi was very calm and got along well with Lorraine's dog, a twelve-year-old Boxer, Bobby, he was still young and had a lot of energy. He kept trying to run around, forgetting that he now had only three legs, and he repeatedly fell and banged his stump on the floor.

In the end, a very distressed Haatchi stayed with Lorraine for only one night.

He spent it crashing around, banging himself and crying out each time, until Lorraine decided that the best place for him right now was back at Harmsworth Hospital . . .

Anatolian Shepherds are relatively rare in the animal-rescue world, so the hospital hoped that, in spite of his many problems, the photographs they had released of Haatchi would be spotted by a kind stranger and that he would be saved.

Luckily, he was.

Haatchi's brand-new life was about to begin.

4

What's Wrong?

Owen Howkins was born on 25 August 2005 in a hospital in Dundee, Scotland.

His birth went normally, and as far as everyone was concerned he was a perfect baby. The only thing his mum, Kim, spotted was that the top of one of his ears had curled in a little — something that most people wouldn't even have noticed.

All the early photographs of Owen show a happy, plump baby. His health visitor assured his parents that he was completely normal.

But as the months passed they began to wonder if he was thriving as well as he should for his age. He seemed to pick up every cold, and he was a hot and sweaty child. Before long he started coughing frequently and then being sick at night.

They tried not to worry, but by the time Owen was eighteen months old, it was clear he wasn't developing completely normally. His cousin Molly was a year younger but Owen looked like the baby next to her.

Will, Owen's dad, and Kim had noticed that their son wasn't crawling so much as dragging himself along. He was also losing his baby fat too quickly and not going to the toilet normally. They took him to the doctor, who examined him and felt tight muscles in his tummy. He gave him some medicine, but it didn't work and Owen continued to lose weight.

Owen's parents and grandparents didn't know if the problem was physical or mental: their baby boy would become very upset if they skipped a verse of one of his favourite nursery rhymes or moved one of his toys out of the perfect row he'd created. Instead of being a bouncing, healthy baby, he was poorly and pale and his nasty cough wouldn't go away.

Will tried to reassure himself that there was nothing wrong, but privately he noticed more and more things Owen was unable to do, and he started to become frightened for his son. Most noticeably, Owen couldn't walk without help; he was using little plastic golf clubs as a way of supporting himself. Will took them away from him to try to get him to walk normally, but he couldn't do it.

As the weeks and months went by, Owen's body began to tighten and his face became pinched to the point where people started staring at him. His family dressed him in a T-shirt whenever they took him swimming so that nobody would notice how different his body looked from other children's. His voice was higher-pitched than normal too, and it was becoming more and more apparent that something wasn't right.

After a lot of tests, Owen and his family were finally given an answer about what was wrong. His curled-in ear as a baby had pointed to the answer.

The doctor wrote something down on a piece of paper and told them that this was what he thought Owen might have. The words he wrote were 'Schwartz-Jampel syndrome'. It was the first the family had ever heard of it.

Getting About

The doctors had never personally come across a case of Schwartz-Jampel syndrome before. They believed that this was the first case of its kind known in the UK; fewer than a hundred cases had ever been reported worldwide.

Dr Thomas, Owen's main doctor, explained that Owen's muscles weren't relaxing after they'd contracted. He said it was a bit like someone shaking your hand and then not being able to let go. Because of this his muscles were becoming increasingly stiff and tight, putting constant pressure on his skeleton. This would eventually stop Owen's bones from growing naturally; he would be smaller than most people and his face muscles would tighten and scrunch up his features, squeezing his eyes shut and pursing his lips. Many of the people who have Schwartz-Jampel syndrome have problems with eyesight, special dental needs and a higher than normal pitch to their voice.

Despite all this, Owen's family were told that he should be able to lead a relatively full life.

The difficulty is that the syndrome affects people in different ways.

At the moment only around thirty people in the world – as far afield as Nepal, Saudi Arabia, the United States and Europe – are known to be living with Schwartz-Jampel syndrome.

The news that Owen had the rare syndrome was shocking. There were far more questions than answers at this first meeting.

The family were told he would almost certainly need frequent physiotherapy to help ease the pressure of his contracted muscles on his skeleton. He might also have to wear splints to stretch his leg muscles, and he could face a series of operations as he grew up. There was a chance that he would spend his later life confined to a wheelchair.

There is no known cure.

Kim and Will bought Owen a walker and tried to coax him into using it by decorating it in the same green as his favourite Ben 10 character. They covered it with lights and stickers, but Owen was still reluctant to use it or to attempt to walk on his own.

His mum was worried that Owen would never splash in the puddles or spend a normal Sunday with a roast dinner followed by an afternoon kicking a ball around the garden with his dad.

And his dad felt the same way. 'You want to see your child run about the park. You want to play football with your son. It hit me very hard then that this was never going to happen.'

They tried to focus on the positives, which wasn't always easy.

Owen had started falling over a lot. Because his muscles never relaxed, it was almost impossible for him to put out his arms to save himself, so he tended to hurt himself whenever he fell. Kim was with Owen in a restaurant when he slipped off a bench and cut his head open. There was blood everywhere, and she had to call an ambulance. Something similar happened at his nursery, and he got a black eye when his grandparents' Springer Spaniel accidentally tripped him up.

'When he falls, he falls like a tree trunk,' noticed Kim. 'Because he can't bend to save himself, despite my dad showing him how to do Commando rolls!' Everyone had to be on constant alert.

Owen had regular physiotherapy and occupational therapy, and his walking frame helped propel him along. In the early days, he'd walk up the hill to nursery and home again. He'd lift his legs on the way home and wheel himself back down the hill.

His parents, who were both in the RAF, bought him a fold-down stool with wheels for home, which made life easier there, but when he went to nursery he tried to keep up with the other children tearing around the playground by running on his toes in his frame.

The family began to organize charity events, including a half-marathon, a pastry-bake, a raffle and a cupcake sale to raise money for a new Zippie wheelchair for Owen to use. Will and Kim will always be grateful for the way their friends and family rallied round to help them, just as they always had.

Little Buddy

Will and Kim decided that as much as they both loved Owen, everybody would be happier if they got a divorce.

After a while Will got a new girlfriend, Colleen, who worked as a dog-trainer. She met Owen for the first time on his fourth birthday and was determined to buy him a birthday gift. She didn't know what he liked, so she asked Will's advice.

'Anything with Ben 10 on it,' he said.

So Colleen went to Toys "R" Us and asked someone to direct her to the Ben 10 aisle, even though she had no idea what it was. She eventually picked out a remote-controlled car because it had a big round controller instead of a stick, which she thought might be better for Owen's hands.

Owen was sitting in his special chair with a little fluffy cushion when Colleen went into the house to meet him, and she thought he was the cutest thing she had ever seen. But she was determined not to overreact or throw herself at him, which she suspected would only scare him. Nor did she want to go rushing in and step on anyone's toes.

'He is Kim's son and she's a perfectly good mother. It is not my job to be his mother. It is my job just to be Colleen.'

'Hello, mate. Happy birthday, little buddy. Can I sit next to you?' she said.

Owen nodded and smiled and let Colleen cuddle up to him.

From that day on Owen had a new nickname: 'Little Buddy' – soon shortened to Little B.

She gave him his present and was amazed by his reaction.

Owen put her gift down on the table and carefully opened his card first, pretending to read it (even though he couldn't yet). Then he opened his present, gently lifting the Sellotape and being careful not to spoil the paper.

The pair got along famously.

The next time Colleen saw 'Little B' it was at Will's parents' house; it was the first time she had met them and she got along with them immediately too. She walked into their lounge, where Owen was playing on the floor, and said, 'Good day, mate, how are you?'

Looking up, he cried out, 'Colleeeen!' and crawled along the furniture to put his arms out to her.

'I just melted in a puddle of Anchor butter,' Colleen remembers.

Colleen was there when Owen fell down the stairs one night, which gave them all a fright.

And even more of a fright when he did it again.

Will and Colleen discovered that Owen had taught himself to flip over in bed and get out of his room because he wanted to walk 'like a big boy'. They could hear his hands tap–tap–tapping on the wall if he came in to see them. Then one day he tried the stairs because he wanted to go down and make breakfast for them as a surprise.

Colleen couldn't bear the idea of Owen falling again. A couple of days later she put her house up for sale and told Will they were buying a bungalow together.

They'd only known each other for a few months but he knew she was right.

Keen to include Owen in every decision that impacted on his life, they took him along to view some places, and when they found the one to which they would eventually move Owen walked in and cried, 'Yay! No stairs!'

The decision was made. They were going to be a family.

★ ★ ★

Owen started at primary school and seemed to be getting along all right with his fellow pupils at first, but after a while his family noticed that he was becoming increasingly withdrawn. Having been protected by them for years, he had suddenly come face to face with children the same age who were happily running around, whereas he could move about only by holding onto the walls. He couldn't stand up by himself and was relying on his walker more and more.

Although Owen was too young to put it into words, he was beginning to realize that there were some things his friends could do now, such as learning how to play football, that he would never be able to do, and he was really taking it to heart. He had always been bright and funny and quite observant, but now he was retreating into himself.

Will wondered what he could do to bring him out of his shell.

He hoped that if Little B could move around more easily then he might not feel quite so left out. He made the tough decision to apply for a wheelchair for Owen from the local health authority, which seemed a huge step.

Unfortunately, the authority ruled that as Owen could occasionally walk (with assistance), he didn't qualify for more than the basic model of wheelchair, which was heavy, ugly and very difficult to manoeuvre.

Owen himself, however, made it easier for everyone by showing great excitement about having what he called a 'bigger, better buggy', even if it was impossible for him to move it by himself and it jolted him badly every time it went over a bump, giving him headaches.

Just as Owen got used to his new wheels and seemed to be making some friends at school, though, he had a growth spurt that caused his spasms to tighten his facial features even more. His eyes started narrowing and his muscles became even more pronounced.

'People really took notice of him, and when he cottoned on to the fact that they were looking at him he began to put his head down. He hated people staring at him, and the more they did, the more he hid away,' Will says.

Before long, Little B no longer wanted to go out in public. Whenever his dad told him they were going to the park or the shops, he'd protest. He hated all the stares he got from people and so he would curl in on himself almost every time he was taken out of his home in his wheelchair.

'People are staring at me!' he complained.

When Will insisted they go out, Owen would beg his dad to carry him instead. It broke Will's heart to tell him he was too heavy for that. He had no choice but to strap his son into the wheelchair and take him out anyway, but Owen hated it and got very upset.

Owen told Kim too: 'People are looking at me and I don't like it!'

At first his mum tried to persuade him that it was because he was 'so adorable'. 'It doesn't mean people don't like you. It's just that you're a little bit different.' But in the end she had to tell her son that some people just didn't understand.

Rock 'n' Roll King

Will had always made a point of including Owen in any decision that would affect him, so he had already asked his son's permission to propose marriage to Colleen. He asked him how he would feel about having Colleen as his step-mum and Owen shouted out, 'Yes!' He had loved her from day one, so he was delighted.

Will also asked Owen if he would do him the honour of being his best man.

'Cool!' Owen replied.

The couple knew they'd need time to save up for the kind of wedding they wanted, so they set the date for the summer of 2013. Colleen's lucky number is seventeen, so they picked the only Saturday the 17th they could find – which happened to fall in August. The whole family was looking forward to the big day.

Little B was doing a bit better at school now, but when he was teased a couple of times he started to lash out.

One day another boy had told him he looked 'funny', so Owen had head-butted him.

Will had to go to the school to talk to his son, who first of all tried to make them believe that the other boy had slipped and hit his head. They had a serious word.

'You can only ever strike out physically if you are struck first,' Will told him.

It hasn't happened since.

No matter how well behaved he was at school

or how comfortable he felt with his family or in a place where he knew everyone, Owen was still very shy, anxious and withdrawn in public and didn't want to be seen.

Everyone, from Will and Colleen to Kim and his grandparents, was growing more and more worried. Owen hardly ever had any friends round to play and he didn't go to other children's homes much either. He was getting impatient at having to put on his leg splints and take his medication.

He was happiest at home watching TV or in a restaurant with his family – his local Pizza Express had become his favourite and he knew exactly what to order every time.

If the family took him anywhere else in public, though, he was patently unhappy. Once, in a supermarket, he challenged an old lady who was staring at him and asked her to stop. When she didn't, he told her she smelled. Will told him that he should always be polite, even if others were being rude, but Owen's growing awareness of his disability and how others viewed him was clearly beginning to affect him.

In the hopes of lifting his spirits, Will arranged a fifth birthday party for his son at the church hall nearby. He told Owen he could have any theme he wanted.

Owen, who often asked to listen to Metallica during breakfast, picked 'Rock 'n' Roll'.

Everyone had to dress up as a rock star. He asked for a bouncy castle so that he could watch his friends having fun.

'He had a fantastic day,' said Will. 'He even went on the bouncy castle and enjoyed being bumped around. I think that was when a lot of the other kids and their parents realized that Little B could party just as hard as they could.'

Will and Colleen decided it might be a good time to get a rescue dog – they both loved dogs. Will had grown up with a Flat-coated Retriever named Jessie, and Colleen already had two working dogs that Will also liked having around. They both hoped that having a dog of his own might be good for Owen. The one they chose was a Spaniel-Collie cross puppy that they named Mr Pixel.

Little B loved Mr Pixel, but he never bonded with him in the way his dad and Colleen had hoped, but nevertheless they set about making a cosy home for Owen, themselves and Mr Pixel (along with Colleen's two dogs, who lived in purpose-built kennels in their garden) in their new bungalow.

Owen was soldiering on, although he now needed a lot of medical help. The muscle contractions in his face were pinching his features and narrowing his eyelids, making it more and more difficult for him to see; the doctors told Will that they might eventually have to operate on the lids in order to keep his eyes open. His eyesight had also deteriorated – partly due to his medication – and he needed glasses now. Owen was also taking part in sleep studies at Southampton Hospital to check his breathing. The spasms in his chest had worsened, which meant that when he lay down to sleep, the tightening muscles crushed his chest and stopped him from breathing easily. This meant he kept waking up to cough – sometimes as many as fifty times in one night. He had also developed asthma because he couldn't fully expand his ribcage.

Owen's doctors prescribed an oxygen mask for him at night, which helped, but Little B didn't like the nasal mask attached to a tube, or the tape required to hold it in place. Will had to set his alarm and get up four or five times a night to check that the mask was still in place or his son might start to choke.

In spite of their hectic lives, Will and Colleen were considering getting a companion for Mr Pixel, and had the idea of rescuing another dog. Although they had to think about it very carefully because of Little B, Colleen knew a great deal about training dogs and how to correct bad behaviour, so she didn't think there was much that she couldn't handle.

One night in January 2012 Colleen was sitting on the sofa next to Will scrolling through the internet searching for a rescue dog when she saw a face looking back at her on the computer and she gasped.

The intense gaze of an Anatolian Shepherd bored straight through her.

Looking up, Will saw Colleen's expression and said, 'Oh no – what have you found?' She didn't say a word – she couldn't speak. She just turned the computer round to face him.

Will took one look at those puppy-dog eyes, and they both instantly realized that he was the one for them. All they knew about him at that point was that his name was Haatchi.

8

The Day That
Everything Changed

Colleen only discovered that Haatchi had lost a leg when she read a little bit more about him. Her chief concern was that his owners might still be looking for him somewhere, but she was assured that it had been weeks since the accident and no one had come forward. Nor was he microchipped, so his family couldn't be traced.

The dog's disability hardly bothered her or Will

at all. They were much more worried about his size and temperament around Little B.

Colleen prayed it would make her little buddy happier to have a big cuddly bear around, and a few days later she went to meet Haatchi at his new foster home, where he was living with lots of other dogs in need.

As Colleen wandered out into the garden with Ross, one of Haatchi's foster dads, her eyes fell first upon Claude, a huge Great Dane who was posing like a statue in the middle of the lawn. She realized that she could see another dog standing behind Claude – on just three legs.

A big head was staring at her from under Claude's belly with those same two piercing eyes that she had seen on the computer screen a few days before.

Colleen gasped and took a massive breath, which she then held on to. She had never felt like this about any dog in her life – ever.

Ross saw that Colleen was in shock and he slapped her on the back. 'Colleen! Breathe!'

Colleen managed to catch her breath and clasped her hand to her chest as she gasped for air.

Ross took her inside to recover and then his partner, James, brought Haatchi in to meet her.

She sat on the sofa as the Anatolian Shepherd staggered in, slipping all over the place because he still hadn't got used to walking on three legs.

Colleen slid to the floor and Haatchi flopped on top of her, tucking his freckle-covered nose into her neck. He seemed very sad, whining and in obvious pain. She recognized that he craved human attention and that he was very confused.

'A dog without a tail has great difficulty in communicating with other dogs, because a tail is such a vital tool of communication in many animals,' Ross told her. 'So really, it's as if Haatchi had lost his voice.'

He also told Colleen that the other dogs didn't really want to make friends with Haatchi because they all found his three legs strange, both to look at and to smell.

To make matters worse, Haatchi also suffered

from what is known as 'ghost limb' syndrome for a while, which meant he thought that his missing leg was still there. He'd try to scratch himself behind the ear with it and only end up jerking his stump before whimpering in frustration and pain.

When he finally settled into Colleen's lap, he rolled onto his back and presented her with his leg stump.

'Can I touch it?' she asked him gently.

Haatchi didn't seem to mind, so she placed her hand on it and discovered that it was really hot.

Haatchi completely curled himself around her.

All of a sudden James nudged Ross and said, 'Look!'

Haatchi's odd little stump of a tail was wagging – the first time he'd moved it since he'd come to live with them. Up until then, they told Colleen, they didn't even know if he could.

From that moment Colleen was sold. 'Haatchi has chosen us!' she cried. She was in love.

When Colleen got home later that night she burst

into tears as she told Will how incredible Haatchi was and how sad she was about what had happened to him. The couple had two weeks to consider whether they were truly prepared to take on such a large three-legged animal. They needed to be sure they were doing the right thing and for the right reasons. Owen was Will's priority. He needed to be convinced that a dog who had suffered so much would be safe around his son, and he told Colleen that if there was even one growl, then Haatchi was out.

Once they'd made their decision to take Haatchi, they had to pass a home check before Colleen would be allowed to collect him. They were a little nervous as their home was inspected and they were asked questions about where Haatchi would be kept and how long he might be left on his own during the day. Only when they were informed that they had passed the home check was Colleen able to drive back to Ross and James's house to pick up the newest member of the family.

Owen has always loved secrets and surprises, so Will and Colleen hadn't told him anything about who was coming to live with them.

He was fast asleep in bed by the time Colleen got home with Haatchi late on the night of 18 February, so they closed his bedroom door and let their new dog limp around the house to explore. Then they introduced him to Mr Pixel. Just as they'd hoped, the two dogs got along well.

After he had explored every corner of their house and worked out where everything was, Haatchi kept returning to sniff at Owen's bedroom door, so they opened it quietly.

Up until that point, Haatchi had been slipping and sliding all over the house and getting overexcited. The moment he stepped into Owen's bedroom, which was decorated with murals of *Star Wars* and *Toy Story*, he completely changed.

As soon as he saw Owen's oxygen mask and the other medical equipment, he sniffed the air repeatedly and almost tiptoed across to where Little B lay.

Will and Colleen watched as he tilted his head, as if to say, 'Hmmm, there's something interesting here.' It was as if he knew this was a vulnerable little boy and that the machinery and tubes were a no-go area for him. Then he silently backed away.

The following morning, Will woke his son at 7 a.m. and sat on the edge of the bed as Owen, looking like a little sleepy slug, rubbed his eyes and yawned.

'There's a big surprise for you!' Will told him.

That made Owen wake up very quickly and become very excited.

Will invited Colleen to bring Haatchi in.

Owen's mouth fell open as a dog three times his size lolloped over and, without any encouragement, placed his head calmly and quietly on Owen's leg. They took one look at each other and melted.

Neither boy nor dog backed away from each other or appeared to be in the least bit fazed. Both seemed to realize that there was something unusual about the other. Haatchi wasn't perfect and he wasn't normal, but Owen could see that, although he was so big, he was just getting on with being disabled and didn't let it bother him.

It was love at first sight – for both of them.

Owen asked what had happened to Haatchi's leg and tail. They didn't want to lie, but it was a hard story both to tell and to hear.

Little B cried as they explained as best they could, while he carried on stroking the dog's big head. Overcome with sadness, he asked why anyone would be so cruel as to abandon such a beautiful dog on a railway line. Will and Colleen told him they didn't know, but assured him that the police would catch the person and tell them off. That made him feel a little better.

He got himself up and into his walker and wandered into the living room.

Haatchi followed devotedly behind.

The two of them curled up together on the sofa, where Owen stroked his new friend some more and began to whisper in his ear. Already they were inseparable, and Will and Colleen both knew that Haatchi was there to stay.

'I felt really happy,' Owen said later with a smile. 'Everything changed in my life that day.'

Best Buddies

Owen was delighted to have a new big brave buddy to huggle, and Haatchi was brilliant to have around.

But Will and Colleen were beginning to realize what was involved in keeping Haatchi fit and healthy. He would need constant monitoring and frequent visits to the vet, all to be fitted in alongside Owen's schooling and medical appointments, plus the pressures of both of them working full-time. It was a sacrifice they were prepared to make, though, just to have the handsome Anatolian Shepherd in their lives.

What they hadn't expected, however, was the change Haatchi brought about in Little B. Suddenly he was so much happier. It was a surprise to everyone.

Owen had become increasingly tricky about taking his medicines. 'I hate the taste!' he told his father. He had also started to argue with Will and Colleen about eating healthy foods – especially green vegetables.

But when Owen saw how good Haatchi was at eating his raw food and taking all his pills, he decided that he would be as brave as his dog.

Watched by his new best buddy, Little B would now line up all his medicines on the table in front of him in a specific order and make sure he got the worst-tasting ones over with first.

'I have to man up!' he told his dad and Haatchi, before swallowing them all down.

Haatchi was at Little B's side whenever he had to go through any painful physiotherapy sessions, always giving Owen a comforting lick from his big pink tongue when it was needed. When he was very excited he'd speak to Owen in his special dog talk that made him sound a bit like Scooby-Doo. And, of course, there were always goodnight huggles before they both went to sleep.

Haatchi loved Owen, and obviously now saw it as his duty to protect his friend. When Owen went back to school the Monday after Haatchi arrived, the dog wandered restlessly around the house looking for his little boy and didn't settle until he came home. It was clear that he was missing his new best friend.

The following day, when Will went to fetch Owen from school, Haatchi sat by the window, his face pressed against the glass, until they returned.

On day three, he took up his position at the window ten minutes before Will even left to collect Little B – and he has done that ever since.

★ ★ ★

During the first few days after Haatchi moved in with them, Will took Owen and the dogs out for their daily walk.

As usual, Owen put on his beanie hat, kept his head down and his hands thrust into pockets. His body curled in on itself, making a confused Haatchi look on and wonder where his little buddy had gone.

One by one, strangers began to notice the unusual dog. Delighted by his size and the fact that he seemed to be coping so well with three legs, people approached to say hello or stroke him, completely ignoring Owen.

Within two weeks of Haatchi's arrival, Little B shocked his father by saying. 'Dad, can we go out for a walk in the snow?'

Will happily agreed and they set off with Haatchi's lead tied loosely to the back of Owen's wheelchair.

People still stared at the unusual family group, but now it was for a different reason. They were admiring the handsome three-legged dog and no longer focusing on the shy little boy in the wheel-chair. Once again, complete strangers approached and asked about Haatchi.

To Will's amazement, and before he could even respond, Owen unexpectedly lifted his head and told them the whole story, talking to strangers for the first time.

The story of how Haatchi lost his leg and tail affected everybody Owen told. Young and old were fascinated by how well Haatchi managed with only three legs, and would almost always tell Owen what a 'cool' dog he had before complimenting him on his 'wheels'.

Everyone in the family noticed the difference in Owen almost straight away.

'At first I thought, "Oh no, not another dog!"' Kim admitted. 'But then I saw how Owen started to change and grow more confident. All he talked about was Haatchi this and Haatchi that. He really came into his own. That dog has been like a miracle.'

For the first time Owen realized that people weren't interested in him or staring at him because he was different but because he had a cool dog. It wasn't too long before he asked Will to bring Haatchi with him when he collected him from school so that his friends could meet him, and he soon made his unusual pet the subject of projects and artwork.

One day Little B did something that neither his family nor his teachers would ever have expected. He stood up in front of a class of younger children and spoke of his ambition to learn to walk again. He announced that he was going to do it with the help of his special dog. He made everybody cry with happiness.

Haatchi had given Owen a newfound confidence that he probably couldn't have got from another human. They acted like a team and they worked together to get through their days.

Haatchi had taught Owen the true meaning of friendship.

10

Friends Around the World

Haatchi was getting better and more healthy by the day, so less than a month after his arrival, Will and Colleen decided to take him and Little B to the famous Crufts dog show at the National Exhibition Centre in Birmingham.

It would be the biggest public outing Owen had ever been on, with several thousand people at the show.

Within hours of their arrival it was obvious to everyone that Haatchi was a massive crowd-pleaser. Just the sight him would stop people in their tracks. Complete strangers would drop to their knees to hug him or even start rolling about with him on the floor.

Neither Will nor Colleen had had any idea that he would have that kind of effect, and they were staggered to see how well the public responded to him.

Owen soon became as popular as his dog, talking to everyone and happily posing for photographs with his new buddy. He even gave some media interviews. Watching him, Will and Colleen could hardly believe this was the same little boy who had previously barely said a word to anyone in public.

'That was the day it all began,' Colleen remembered. 'It was as if Little B had been a bud waiting for the light and love of Haatchi to make him flower. Haatchi made it possible for the whole world to know what a beautiful and remarkable little boy Owen Howkins really is.'

★ ★ ★

Back home after Crufts, Haatchi was still learning how best to manage with a missing leg. His remaining three had to work much harder than usual. He had a little leather boot made for his rear paw to give it extra grip, which especially helped when he tried to stand up.

Will and Colleen had installed wood flooring for Owen, because it meant he could move about more easily in his walking frame and wheelchair. But polished floors were not ideal for a growing tri-paw doggy like Haatchi.

Ever the survivor, though, it didn't take Haatchi long to get the hang of his new home. He even figured out how to get his enormous body through the small dogflap the couple had installed in the back door for Mr Pixel, pushing his head and shoulders through, sending the plastic flap flying!

It wasn't long after Crufts that Haatchi's incredible story went viral. He began to be featured in local and national media, and gifts and treats started arriving for him and Little B in the mail.

Owen had always loved receiving postcards – ever since Colleen's mother, Kathryn, had sent him one all the way from New Zealand – so he was very excited to get even more from his and Haatchi's many fans around the globe. One American family from Idaho sent him a fabric map of the world, so Will created a padded 'postcard map' out of it to hang on Owen's wall and mark off each new country. The UK and Europe quickly filled up with coloured pins, so the more exotic the postmark, the better. Will even set up a special PO box for Owen so that their postman could cope!

Crufts had been such a success that Will and Colleen started to attend other dog shows with Haatchi and Little B. Over the course of the next few months, they went to events such as Bark in the Park, Discover Dogs, Paws in the Park, and many other charity shows. Each outing proved to be great fun, with Haatchi and Owen getting lots of attention and the Anatolian Shepherd winning all sorts of prizes for anything from 'Best Rescue' to 'Best Friend'. Owen loved showing him off.

During the 2012 London Olympics, Will took three weeks off work to stay at home with Owen so that they could watch it on TV every day. Little B was even allowed to stay up for the opening ceremony, his arm around Haatchi's neck throughout the whole thing.

Then the Paralympics began, and Will noticed how fascinated and impressed his son was by all those who had overcome their disabilities to become inspirational sportsmen and -women. He managed to get them seats at a few of the events. They took Owen's cousin, Molly, along to watch a round of bocce (which is like boules or pétanque but played with soft balls).

Little B loved those games and was completely gripped by the whole event.

Will believed it taught him a great deal about

being independent and becoming his own man, regardless of the fact that he was in a wheelchair. He could see just how normal disabled people's lives can be.

11

It's Not How Many Legs or Wheels; it's Who Journeys with You

In September 2012 Owen was due to start at junior school – at a place that not only was wheelchair friendly but had been carefully selected to allow him to be treated just like everybody else.

With none of his primary-school classmates moving with him and the help of only two special needs assistants, who'd take turns to do morning and afternoon shifts, everyone was worried about how the still sometimes shy little boy would respond in a strange new environment.

Keen to help Little B all she could, especially when it came to keeping up with his schoolmates, Colleen came up with a plan to raise money for a state-of-the-art electric wheelchair for him to use at his new school.

One night she had a dream. 'I was wheeling Owen around in his horrible NHS wheelchair but there was a coin slot in the arm. As we walked, people came up and put £1 coins into the slot. Each time they did, the wheelchair morphed into something better and better until it became a top-of-the-range electric one.'

Colleen woke up early the next morning and told Will she was going to do a £1 wheelchair walk to raise the money they would need for Owen's new chair. She figured that if all their friends donated £1, they could at least raise enough for the deposit. Her aim was to walk from Southampton Hospital to their home town of Basingstoke, a distance of thirty-one miles, in a day.

Donations flooded in and the walk was planned for December 2012. They raised the money they needed just in time!

In preparation for the walk, Colleen and Will had T-shirts made up, which read: NEVER WALK ALONE. The back said: IT'S NOT HOW MANY LEGS OR WHEELS. IT'S WHO JOURNEYS WITH YOU.

A friend made a batch of special Haatchi cakepops with his face on for them to eat and give away while they walked, and lots of other friends and family members joined them on the walk and came to cheer them on.

Haatchi and Little B were waiting for them at the end, at Basingstoke Hospital.

The walk was a huge success.

Owen's brand-new wheelchair was unveiled to him as a surprise during a normal visit to collect Haatchi's special food from the shop.

His dad filmed the moment when Owen was

invited to pull off the white sheet covering the chair, and he managed to get close-ups of Little B gasping at the sight of his stunning new wheels.

Painted electric blue and with four-wheel drive so it could go off road, the new machine had lights and indicators as well as a roll-bar, horn, racing seatbelts and a personalized number plate spelling Owen.

After his first spin around the block (Haatchi at his side, of course), Little B grinned and gave his new chair the thumbs-up. 'Totally awesome!'

A Hug from Haatchi

On Little B's first day at his new school, Will and Colleen took Haatchi along in the back of the car so that Owen could show him off.

The sight of the furry three-legged dog attracted a lot of interest!

Owen's new school friends loved meeting Haatchi, and the big dog wiggled his body and spoke to them in his Scooby-Doo language, which made them giggle.

71

Will and Colleen left Owen in the care of his new teacher, hoping for the best, but seeing how Haatchi responded to the children gave Colleen an idea. She was going to train Haatchi as a therapy dog – a dog who could give love and comfort to people in need.

The difference Haatchi had made to Owen's life had been nothing short of a miracle, and rather than taking it for granted or keeping it to themselves, Colleen wanted to make the same feel-good factor available to other people.

When he eventually came home from school later that day, Owen was crying. He immediately buried his head in Haatchi's neck.

Scared that someone had picked on his son, Will asked, 'What's wrong?'

'I don't like all the girls calling me cute!' Little B sobbed.

Will and Colleen tried not to laugh.

They discovered that when the girls at school told Little B he was cute, he thought they were commenting on the fact that he was smaller than the other boys in the class.

It took a while to calm Owen down as Will explained that 'cute' wasn't anything bad at all. 'I wish the girls at my school had thought I was cute!' he told his son.

Within a short space of time Owen was loving his new school – he made a group of friends who loved his cheeky fun and became very protective of him.

His two special needs assistants, Miss O'Hagan and Mrs Hayward, took turns to help him do the things he couldn't manage, such as using the toilet or reaching something, but made sure that Owen still had some independence.

Like his dad, Owen enjoyed all things technological and did especially well at maths, literacy and art, as well as reading and French. But like lots of children he still had to be reminded to behave, do his homework, eat his vegetables and not stay up too late on school nights playing his computer games!

Haatchi had to be told off occasionally too!

Although he loved people and was good with strangers, behaving well even at busy shows, his Anatolian guard-dog roots meant that he had taken to barking at anyone who walked past the house – especially when he was pressing his nose against the window waiting for Owen. He wanted to protect his family and so he would also bark at any dog – especially a nervous or aggressive one – that he saw as a possible threat. As his bark was so loud, it was usually enough to frighten them away.

Haatchi's training as one of the UK's five thousand Pets As Therapy dogs began when he was only a few months old. After he had passed the test, Colleen taught him some basic commands, such as 'Sit' and how to take a treat politely.

He was a natural at both.

Then Colleen started to make loud noises near the dog – including popping balloons, dropping heavy objects and ringing bells – to make sure he reacted calmly.

Haatchi never made a fuss and responded in his usual laid-back way.

During Haatchi's training, Colleen found out that a little girl Haatchi had met at one of the shows he'd been to with Owen was very sick. She was going into hospital to have a big operation.

She asked the girl's parents if it might cheer her up if Haatchi went to visit her.

They agreed at once.

As Haatchi was still doing his training, he wasn't officially counted as a therapy dog, but Colleen drove Haatchi to the hospital to meet his friend anyway. She thought that even seeing Haatchi from the window of her ward might cheer the little girl up.

As they stood outside the entrance of the hospital, the doorway quickly became blocked with people wanting to pet Haatchi and say hello, and the kind hospital staff said it was OK for Haatchi to come inside and say hi to his friend.

'OK, buddy, let's see how you cope with this!' Colleen took a deep breath.

Inside, the floors were very shiny, but Haatchi managed to walk on them, and when he got to the ward he went straight to the girl's cubicle and quietly nuzzled her hand, just as he had when he first met Owen.

Her parents had to stop her jumping out of bed to throw her arms around Haatchi's neck.

An Almost Disaster

Within a year of being rescued, Haatchi had become so used to his three legs that he could keep up with Mr Pixel.

The family was booked to go back to Crufts in March to support all the new friends they had made over the past year, so they were especially delighted when they heard some more good news for Haatchi.

Their wonderful dog had been nominated for

the very special Friends for Life Award, which would be decided by a public vote. He had been picked for the final from more than twenty thousand dogs. The other four finalists were all brilliant so it was going to be a tough choice for the judges! They were:

- Brin, an abandoned Afghani stray, who had barked to alert two soldiers to a roadside bomb that would have killed them.
- Janus, a Belgian Malinois, who had made more than four hundred arrests as a police dog.
- Daisy, a Bull Mastiff, who had helped a family recover from the loss of their six-year-old son.
- Max and Ziggy – two assistance dogs – who had helped their owners find love.

Owen was super pleased that his dog had been nominated and even more excited when – because they had been brought to public attention – he and Haatchi were invited to appear on *This Morning* with Holly Willoughby and Phillip Schofield.

On the day of their TV appearance, Owen held his head high and gave a huge smile.

'I used to be scared of strangers, then Haatchi came along and now I'm not,' Owen told the cameras. 'I didn't really meet many others with disabilities and felt like the odd one out, which made me really sad. But then I saw Haatchi and I saw how strong he was, even though he only had three legs. I became stronger myself. I love him so much.'

Holly and Phillip loved meeting Owen and Haatchi, and wished him all the best for Crufts.

The organizers of the famous dog show created a short video of each of the finalists so that the public could choose which one they wanted to win.

Owen sat on the sofa next to his special dog, hugged him and introduced 'my best friend Haatchi'.

The video touched so many people.

Afterwards, the Duchess of York sent a toy Buckingham Palace Corgi, and lots of other well-wishers sent cards and toys, treats and sweets.

But then disaster struck.

A month before the family was due to go to Crufts to find out how many people had voted for Haatchi, on a frosty February night, he playfully chased Mr Pixel out of the house through the giant dogflap.

Then came a big bang and the sound of Haatchi whimpering in pain.

Out in the garden, he had slipped on some black ice.

They all rushed out to find Haatchi lying on the ground looking up at them pitifully.

Scared he might have broken his back, Will and Colleen helped the massive dog inside, wrapped him in towels and laid him on his big padded bed with his favourite fluffy toy, Harold Hedgehog.

The vet came and examined him. 'He must have done the splits!' he said.

Poor Haatchi had torn his abductor, stomach and pectoral muscles. He had also damaged his back leg and strained his front ones. Ouch!

Haatchi barely moved for two days.

Owen lay on his bed and hugged his poorly friend whenever he could.

Will and Colleen often caught them having private whispered conversations that Little B made clear were strictly between a boy and his dog. He knew what it was like to feel pain – he'd known it all his life – and just as the two of them had always accepted each other's differences, now they were a team working together to overcome the problems they faced.

Even after the swelling in Haatchi's torn muscles went down, the family was warned it would take several weeks for him to recover. He could have no outside walks at all to begin with, and then only limited exercise for several weeks, if not months.

Haatchi became miserable at being stuck in the house. He would howl whenever Will or Colleen went out for a walk with Mr Pixel or the other dogs and would sit in the window crying.

It was heartbreaking.

Using a harness they had bought to help lift him to his feet and support his weight, Will eventually let the big dog potter about on the front lawn on a lead. Then, as his injuries slowly began to heal, Haatchi was allowed as far as the next house to sniff their grass. As he got better and better he was allowed to explore further.

Haatchi wasn't completely better, but he was well enough to go to Crufts in March with Owen and meet many more of his fans.

He spent a lot of time at the show being patted and hugged in between posing for photographs with Little B.

Then it was time for Haatchi and his proud family to hear the announcement of which dog had won the Friends for Life Award.

All five finalists and their owners were invited into the main arena.

Will and Colleen helped Haatchi and Owen take their place in the spotlight as TV presenter Clare Balding stepped forward to introduce the award. The short films for each nominee were shown, and then they were each interviewed live for the BBC.

'Haatchi made me more confident,' Owen said softly into the microphone as the TV lights dazzled him. Then he clammed up completely, giving everyone a glimpse of the shy little boy he had once been.

The lights were dimmed, the head judge opened a special envelope and announced, 'The winner of Friends for Life, with fifty-four per cent of the vote, is – Owen and Haatchi!'

A huge cheer went up from the crowd. Owen's face broke into an enormous grin, and Will leaned forward to hug and kiss his son.

They were presented with a special crystal vase and then the television crews lined up to interview Owen as he cradled the prize in his lap.

With Haatchi sitting calmly at his side, the little boy – who would have been terrified of speaking like this a year earlier – lifted his head, beamed at the cameras, and said: 'It feels brilliant to win. I'm really happy I got this. I want to thank all of you for voting for me.' He added that Haatchi was 'the brilliantest dog in the world', and said finally,

'I am more than happy. I am mega–mega-*mega* happy!'

The pair won £1,500 to give to the charity of their choice and they picked a children's hospice called Naomi House near their home.

Owen was also presented with some Olympics badges because he'd so loved watching the Paralympics with his dad. 'I'd really like to be a Paralympian one day,' he announced.

Ending what had been an incredible couple of days, Will proudly pushed Little B on a victory lap of the arena as he waved to the clapping crowd, a big grin on his face.

14

More Miracles

Haatchi and Little B were starting to get used to their fame and went on some more TV shows, but there was even more exciting news to come for the best friends.

They were invited to go the British Animal Honours awards ceremony, presented by animal lover and TV presenter Paul O'Grady. The awards honour the UK's most extraordinary animals and the people who dedicate their lives to them. Haatchi had won the show's special Braveheart Honour.

When the day came to film the awards show, Haatchi was helped around the studio by Will and Colleen using his special lifting harness.

Paul O'Grady introduced the winners of the Braveheart Award with the words: 'Sometimes when you see two friends together, it is hard to imagine them ever being apart, but in the case of Owen and Haatchi they very nearly didn't meet at all.'

The audience was shown a short film depicting Haatchi's terrible night on the railway tracks and told, 'There was a good chance that Haatchi would never survive his injuries.'

Rupert Grint, the actor who played Ron Weasley in the Harry Potter films, presented Haatchi with his Braveheart medal as he and Little B received a standing ovation from the studio audience.

When Paul O'Grady saw the audience reaction to the boy and his dog, he told Owen: 'Look at that! You got them all on their feet! They didn't do that for me!' And he praised Owen's suit and tie before getting down on all fours to say a proper hello to Haatchi.

Owen met lots of famous people that night, including the rock star Brian May and his wife, Anita Dobson; Dame Kelly Holmes; and Bob, the cat from the bestselling book *A Street Cat Named Bob*, and his owner James Bowen.

Haatchi was fit and well, but the injuries from his slip on the ice in February were taking much longer to heal than anyone had expected. By April, it was clear that something wasn't right with Haatchi's one remaining back leg.

Colleen and Will decided to take Haatchi to a specialist veterinary surgeon. Before they left, Owen gave Haatchi a huge hug.

The vet, Andy Moores, investigated and found that Haatchi's back leg would need a big operation: he would have to break and straighten his bones. It would be risky for Haatchi and very expensive for Will and Colleen.

Will had given up his job to be able to spend

more time being a great dad for Owen and so he was worried about how he would find the money Haatchi needed.

But the next day, a miracle arrived.

Andy the vet called Will to tell him that he would operate on Haatchi for less money than it would normally cost, and much of that would be paid for by *Dogs Today* magazine as part of a prize for Haatchi.

Once again, the incredible spirit of Haatchi had somehow helped him to overcome the odds.

'We will for ever be indebted to everyone's kindness, generosity and professionalism,' said Will. 'Yet again, Haatchi seemed to bring out the best in people.'

The day of Haatchi's operation came, and Will and Colleen drove him to the vet's early in the morning with Harold Hedgehog at his side.

The front door opened and a vet nurse came out with a dog whose belly was shaved and whose rear leg was bandaged.

Haatchi's nose shot up and he began to whimper. He must have been having a flashback to his painful time at Harmsworth hospital and his first night in the care of the RSPCA all those months ago. Colleen wondered if he might even try to make a run for it.

But then the door opened again and Andy, Haatchi's surgeon, came out and ruffled the dog's ears playfully. They followed him inside and then all the way to the surgical kennels, passing lots of staff who greeted their superstar dog with warm smiles and kind hands.

When they entered the kennel quarters, Andy directed them towards a large cage filled with fluffy white blankets. Haatchi was surrounded by other dogs in smaller kennels, but he didn't bark at any of them. He just sniffed at them suspiciously.

As he approached his cage, Haatchi suddenly froze in his tracks and appeared to be hit by another wave of fear.

Colleen buried her face in his neck and kissed both his ears to calm him down a little.

They finally managed to get him into his kennel and then they placed Harold Hedgehog next to his nose.

Haatchi sniffed the fluffy toy, which had spent the previous night being snuggled in bed by Owen, and seemed comforted by the familiar smell – so much so that they were able to close the kennel door and leave him in Andy's care.

Back home Owen was unusually quiet without his big buddy and hardly said a word as they waited for news.

But when Andy rang to say that the five hours of surgery had gone well and there were no side-effects from the anaesthetic, Little B punched the air with his tiny fist and cried, 'Yay!'

Andy promised that he and his team would look after Haatchi carefully overnight and ring the family back in the morning.

The following day the nurses reported that Haatchi had managed to eat some food after a good night's sleep and was able both to walk (with the help of a sling) and to move his rear leg.

Haatchi had pulled through again.

After that Colleen and Will took turns to visit Haatchi in his kennel at the rehabilitation centre and give him enough cuddles to last him until their next visit.

The big dog hated having to wear a fabric collar to stop him licking his wounds, but he was sleepy from his pain medication and soon dozed off, snoring, in their laps.

Back home, their bungalow seemed empty without Haatchi. Owen asked after him every day and the house just wasn't the same without his enormous, calming presence.

Haatchi's little friend didn't rush in from school like he used to, and was definitely quiet, not even wanting to play his favourite Nerf gun game with his dad, and going to bed early.

Will and Colleen were reminded of the quiet days before Haatchi had come into their lives.

Five days after his operation, Haatchi finally had the one visitor he was most looking forward to seeing.

Under strict supervision so that he didn't move too suddenly or do anything to damage his leg, Haatchi rolled around the lawn with his best friend Owen.

The big dog lit up in Little B's presence as he placed a front leg firmly over Owen's body and pulled him towards him in a smiling, panting huggle.

Cuddles from staff were all right.

Cuddles from Colleen and Will were always welcome.

But nobody cuddled Haatchi like Owen, and the two of them pressed their heads together and stared into each other's eyes with nothing but love.

15

Small Miracles and Big Dreams

Over the next few weeks Haatchi continued to make progress, and the whole family climbed into his cage with him or helped him out on to the back lawn of the recovery centre for playtime.

Haatchi was allowed home for the first time on the May Bank Holiday weekend, to lie in a huge wooden kennel or 'bedroom', especially built by Will (with a lot of help from Owen).

Little B kicked off his shoes and got inside with his furry friend. He was soon snuggled down on Haatchi's bed, demanding a bedtime story.

In the following weeks Haatchi continued to get better and so was allowed another weekend home with Owen, Will and Colleen.

Veterinary staff said that Haatchi's recovery had soared since he'd been reunited with Owen and they were keen for his improvement to continue.

And things did seem to be going brilliantly . . .

Haatchi and Little B made the front page of the June edition of *Dogs Today* magazine (as well as an inside spread). They had been hired as 'roving reporters' for *Dogs Today* and had already written their first blog about their progress called 'Small Miracles and Big Dreams'.

Will and Colleen were two months away from their wedding and looking forward to the big day.

Haatchi was still making good progress and the fur was growing back on his 'baldy bot-bot'.

Owen was still doing well at school – especially in maths – and feeling a little better physically because the summer heat eased his joint pain.

And the family's many friends and well-wishers from all over the world continued to send them surprise gifts, including Lego and a memory-foam bed for Haatchi, plus stickers and magnets, books and sweets for Owen.

But then came some bad news.

Haatchi's latest X-rays showed that although most of his leg was healing, his kneecap was still slipping out of place. Unless Will, Colleen and his therapy teams could build up his muscles with physiotherapy and hydrotherapy to keep the patella stable, Haatchi would need more big operations.

Now the family had to hope and pray that the dog that had changed their lives could have his own happy ending too.

Haatchi's devoted team of veterinary staff started daily therapy sessions to improve Haatchi's muscle strength so that he wouldn't have to undergo any more surgery.

To encourage Haatchi, Will put on some goggles

and a wetsuit to climb into the pool with Haatchi for hydrotherapy.

Swimming so often meant that Haatchi was getting stronger and faster every day. Within weeks he was able to swim by himself and without tipping over for the first time since his operation.

Haatchi was growing bored of being in his cage when he wasn't having therapy, though, and needed to be distracted.

Will and Colleen made up all sorts of games with him that didn't involve much movement – using balls and towels, toys and chews that they could toss around his cage or play tug-of-war with. They moved him from his cage to the lawn, where a physiotherapist, Kate Vardy, massaged him.

Little B did his bit too, spending hours with his dog in and out of his cage – even reading and doing his homework next to his furry friend or using him as a backrest.

As Haatchi nuzzled and tickled Owen, making him laugh, Colleen took dozens of photographs of them, along with some of Haatchi wearing his beloved Harold Hedgehog on his head, rolling on his back or giving Owen a tongue bath.

No one had any idea when Haatchi's real birthdate was, but his first vet had told Will and Colleen that judging from his teeth he must have been approximately seven months old when they got him, which meant he was born some time in July 2011. As seventeen is Colleen's lucky number, they decided to set the date as 17 July, so that his second birthday would fall exactly one month before their wedding day, which was on 17 August.

It was around this time that Owen started to complain that his hips were hurting. His father knew that, because of the medicine he was already taking daily, Little B must really be in pain if he was feeling something new.

Will and Colleen took him back to Southampton General Hospital for some tests, including X-rays of his hips and scans of his whole lower body.

The deterioration in Owen's bones looked as bad as Haatchi's had been.

To keep Little B fully informed, he was allowed into the hospital's radiography room to look at the scans and watch the 3D images of his hip joints panning up on the screen.

As Will and Colleen looked on in silence, they saw for the first time that both Owen's hips were dislocated due to the pressure of the muscles contracting around them, and one of the joints had been worn down to half its normal size.

As he looked at the black-and-white images of his seven-year-old son's skeleton condition, Will realized how brave Owen had been. 'Anyone else would have been crying out in pain, but Owen has a much higher threshold than normal.'

This all meant that later in his life, Owen might well become less mobile and need some operations. For now, he would need some special injections every six months, which would have to be given under general anaesthetic. The date for the first one was booked for August – one week after Will and Colleen's wedding.

Little B had already been through so much in

his short life, but he had coped with it all because of the love and support of his family – and Haatchi. Now, he faced even bigger challenges.

Back home, Little B crawled into the kennel where his beloved Haatchi was still recovering from the big operation to his leg. Owen had seen the way his dog had coped with the pain and frustration of the previous few weeks and wanted to do the same. In one of their many secret conversations as they huggled together gently, Owen told his best buddy that he might have to have surgery as well.

By the time he was sleepily ready for his bed, Little B had decided that he and Haatchi would work through their problems together – just as they always had.

Trains

Fortunately, the family had something wonderful to look forward to – a summer wedding.

From the day he asked Colleen to be his bride, Will had been determined to include Owen in every bit of their wedding plans. He had even got Owen's opinion on the engagement ring. They wanted it to be as much his day as theirs.

Their marriage wouldn't change much about their everyday lives, except that Colleen would officially become Owen's stepmother.

'It must be confusing for a child from a broken home whose mother is away working a lot, but thankfully we hit it off right from the start,' Colleen said.

Only once did Owen ask Colleen if he could call her 'Mum'.

'No, Owen, you've already got a mum,' Colleen gently told him.

Colleen thought it was important that Owen knew that Kim being his mother was not something for her to give up or for Colleen to take on. 'Kim is the reason he is here and I will always be eternally grateful to her for that.'

The couple began to search for a wedding venue where they could have the ceremony and the reception all in the same place. They took Owen with them to view possible sites. They needed it to be as flat as possible so that he had easy access and could use his walker and his wheelchair. It had to be within easy driving distance of either Basingstoke or Southampton Hospitals in case he was taken poorly. Ideally, it should also be near their bungalow so that they wouldn't have to deal with installing an oxygen machine if they stayed over.

In the end they decided on a friendly pub in a converted watermill on the banks of the River Loddon in Old Basing, fifteen minutes from their home. It had a lake and there was an old-fashioned restaurant attached, and the pub gardens were close to a red-brick Victorian viaduct that crossed the river and would provide the perfect backdrop for photographs. It was also mainly on one level, so it seemed perfect, but Will and Colleen were still concerned about the cost.

When they took Owen and Haatchi to see it for the first time, the owners were so taken with them all that they offered the venue at a discount, which meant they could book it. This would be the place for the wedding!

Sitting out on the front lawns having a drink together to celebrate finally having found the perfect location for their wedding, Will, Colleen and Little B couldn't have been happier.

Haatchi lay alongside them quite happily too, but suddenly he sat up, tensed his muscles and started trembling all over.

Colleen and Will noticed it immediately and wondered if he had eaten something that upset him.

But as she went to stroke him, Colleen heard something that made her blood run cold.

'Oh, no!' she cried. 'It's a train. A train's coming across the bridge! He can hear it!'

Ever since they'd rescued Haatchi they had been careful never to take him to a train station or near a railway line in case he suffered some sort of flashback.

As a dog trainer, Colleen knew that the way they handled the next few minutes would be vital to Haatchi's future. Turning away from the cowering animal, she said under her breath to Will and Owen, 'Whatever you do, don't look at him and don't react!'

Deeply concerned for their beloved pet, it took all their willpower not to reassure Haatchi as he quivered and quaked at the sound of the approaching train that must have reminded him of that cold night in January when he'd almost died.

Out of the corner of her eye, Colleen saw Haatchi look anxiously from her to Will to Little B as the train passed directly overhead. His ears were flat and his stump of a tail was firmly tucked down.

But as they all held their breath, the train rumbled past and Haatchi finally stopped shaking. Then he tilted his head quizzically as he registered with apparent surprise that not only was he still alive but that none of his family seemed to be in the slightest bit afraid.

Looking up at them as if to say, 'Hey, nothing happened!' he seemed to shrug his doggie shoulders before slumping back down on the grass to lick his paws, confident that he was safe.

It was a scary moment – for all of them. It was also a very emotional one. In his fear, Haatchi could easily have run from the noise, which would have hurt his leg. He was so big now that they would never have been able to hold him if he'd really wanted to flee.

But Haatchi had trusted them to keep him from harm, and they had.

A Day of Tears and Laughter

When they'd first decided to get married, Colleen and Will thought that as they already had everything they needed, instead of presents they would ask their friends and family if they might like to contribute to a special holiday for Owen.

They had come up with the idea of visiting Santa Claus in Lapland, and decided to have a special secret postbox at their wedding reception for people to drop their contributions into. The whole thing was to be a huge surprise for Little B, so everyone was sworn to secrecy.

Will chose to spend what he jokingly referred to as his 'last night of freedom' alone with Owen. They went to the cinema to see the movie *Planes* and then they ate a burger together before going home to bed. Kissing his son goodnight, Will reflected on how far they had come and how lucky they were to have Colleen and Haatchi in their lives.

Colleen and Will's long-awaited wedding day, Saturday 17 August, dawned grey and cloudy, but nothing could dampen their spirits.

Will helped Owen dress in his little morning suit, then they fixed a newly plaited purple-and-white collar around Haatchi's huge neck.

Will could tell that his son was nervous, so he was pleased he had something to distract him. Once he was in his suit, he presented Little B with his first proper watch as a gift for being best man.

'Awesome!' Owen said, giving his dad a high

five. Squinting at it through his glasses, he admired its stylish black rubber design and magnified face, and for the rest of the day proudly offered to tell the time to anyone who was interested.

In the weeks before the wedding the couple had taken Haatchi back to the venue several times to make sure that he was fully used to the sound of passing trains, so by now the big dog was fine.

'Each time he heard a train approaching,' Will said, 'he'd look up, cock his head, check out our reaction and settle back down when he saw that there was none. He's a smart dog and he figured it out all by himself.'

In the picturesque setting of the watermill, with its industrial cogs and wheels, Will and Colleen said their wedding vows in front of their friends and family.

Soon after they began Haatchi suddenly barked loudly and pawed first the table and then Colleen.

'He wasn't used to seeing me all dressed up,' she said later. 'And he certainly wasn't used to seeing me crying. I think when he heard my voice he suddenly realized that the lady in the dress was me and he wanted some attention.'

Owen took photographs on his grandmother Joan's camera, propped up in his walker in the aisle. He also kept checking the time on his new watch. Will had given him a military-style timetable of when everything would happen and how long each segment would take, and so Owen wanted to be sure that everything was running on time.

He kept the wedding rings in a little velvet bag in a special pocket deep within his waistcoat, and he got them out and looked at them numerous times before and during the ceremony, checking that they were still safe. When his time came he solemnly handed over the rings one by one on cue, looking proudly up at his dad.

After the ceremony, the happy couple went outside to chat to their guests and sip champagne before their meal.

While they were busy mingling, Little B spoke to camera for the wedding video. Taking a deep breath, he smiled, looked straight into the lens like a professional, and said: 'Dear Colleen and Daddy, I'm sending you this message to say congratulations and well done. I love you so much and I can't even believe you got married!'

The wedding photographer asked the bride and groom if he could take some shots of them under the red-brick Victorian railway viaduct.

'Yes, but I think we'll keep Haatchi out of these ones,' Colleen insisted, as she watched her three-legged rescue dog comfortably settled by the fireplace. Knowing that he was safe and happy, she and Will wandered off down a winding gravel path to have the photographs taken to mark their special day.

Will fed Haatchi and arranged for a friend to take him home and put him into his special 'bedroom' before the evening celebrations began.

Little B kissed his big buddy goodnight and went back to having fun.

Apart from the excitement of the day, his new watch and being best man, his big distraction was that – for the first time – he had learned how to blow bubbles. Colleen had put mini champagne bottles filled with bubbles on every table. The plastic containers were small enough for Owen to use. Gripping them in his hands, Little B never tired of dipping a wand in and out, before bringing it close to his eyes to check it was filled with soapy liquid and blowing. He didn't stop even when the music started later. Everyone gathered around to listen, and Little B wheeled his walker closer so that he could sway in time to the music while he blew even more bubbles.

Later, after Will and Colleen's first dance, Owen joined them to dance in their arms to the one song he'd personally requested, 'I Gotta Feeling' by the Black Eyed Peas.

One of the last to leave with Will and Colleen, Owen could hardly keep his eyes open as his father carried his little man out to a waiting taxi.

Suddenly, someone sitting outside the mill house spotted them leaving and cried out: 'Hey! That's the kid off the telly, isn't it? He's famous!'

'Yes he is!' Colleen replied proudly.

The fan quickly rushed over and asked for Owen's autograph. Mustering a sleepy smile, Little B said, 'You'll have to be quick. I'm very tired,' before signing his name.

The new little family finally headed home to a waiting Haatchi after a day that had been full of tears and laughter.

18

Manning Up

After all the joy and excitement of their wedding, the only cloud on their horizon was the latest news about Owen's hips. Two days before their honeymoon began, Will and Colleen had to take him back to Southampton Hospital for the injections that doctors hoped would ease his hip pain.

Before Owen left home for the procedure, Haatchi gave him extra-special cuddles and a 'bravery booster' – lifting his front paw and pulling Little B to him, so that their heads were pressed together and they were looking into each other's eyes. It was as if Haatchi was reassuring him that everything would be all right.

Once Owen was under anaesthetic (cuddling his favourite soft white bear, which reminded him of Haatchi), his doctors were able to administer the injection into his left hip and then examine him more closely. He came round after the operation without remembering anything of what had happened; and he wasn't in too much pain.

Taken to a children's ward to recover, he was looked after by Colleen until a nurse came to remove the two plastic tubes that had been inserted into the veins in his arm.

Knowing that he had to 'man up', Owen asked if he could remove the sticking plasters himself, so Colleen and the nurse soaked them in water in the hope that they wouldn't hurt quite so much when he peeled them off.

When it came to removing the tubes, Little B

looked at Colleen fearfully and told her, 'I really wish this didn't have to happen today.'

Squeezing his hand, she told him she really wished it didn't too.

Looking around the room at the other children lying quietly in their beds, Owen took his new stepmother firmly by the hand and told her, 'Can you please put your hand over my mouth if I scream, so that it doesn't upset the other children?'

When it came to it, Owen couldn't stop himself from screaming. But it was over quickly, and within a few minutes he was sitting up in bed playing his favourite computer game.

He was so involved in it that when they asked him if he would like a bath to scrub off the pen marks on his legs before he went home, he replied: 'I'm in the middle of a war at the moment, so I can't help you.'

While Owen carried on playing his game, Will and Colleen met with the medical staff who had examined him. They learned that there was even more damage to Owen's bones than they had first thought and that if the injections didn't help Owen and he was still in pain, their only other option would be to cut a little bit off the top of his leg bones to stop them from being ground against his other bones and wearing down. This would mean that Owen would almost certainly be permanently confined to a wheelchair, because there wouldn't be enough bone left in his legs to support his weight – especially as he grew bigger and heavier.

This news came as a big shock.

Although most people saw Owen in a wheelchair when he was out in public, at home he either used his walker to get around or used chairs and tables for support. This meant that he could take himself off to his bedroom, the bathroom or to hug Haatchi without help.

Determined to make the most of Owen's eighth birthday, Will and Colleen threw a small party for friends and family, and they all watched as he opened his presents and cards. His new Nerf gun with automatic triggers which were easier for his hands to use, was a big hit, along with some Lego, a hover target and laser gun, and a set of bocce balls just like those he'd watched at the Paralympics with his dad.

Only when Owen's birthday had been properly celebrated did Will and Colleen open all their wedding-day cards to see how much they'd managed to raise for their surprise trip to Lapland with Little B in December. They had a lot! And so they booked the trip.

The family would have a chalet of their own on the reindeer farm rather than staying at a nearby hotel with everyone else, to avoid having to move Owen around too much. And Little B would be able to go out with the dog team and take part in the snowmobile safari like all the other children.

Owen's stiffening joints suffer badly in the cold, so he would need to be kept warm at all times, but the travel company promised they would provide thermal clothing for them all.

Will and Colleen planned on keeping it a surprise from Owen right up until they got him aboard the plane. They just looked forward to seeing his face when he finally set eyes on Father Christmas. It was going to be the perfect end to the year: they could hardly wait.

19

Haatchi in His Forever Home

Lifting his head, he sniffed the air with his wet black nose. He thought he heard a noise but wasn't sure what it was, so he slumped back down where he lay. Peering right and left through amber eyes, he wondered where his humans had gone and why he was alone in the dark.

Would someone come soon?

He heard another noise and his tail stump

twitched. It was coming from Owen's room. Then the overhead light flicked on. Through the cage of his special bedroom built into the dining room of his forever home, he could see his beloved mum approaching in her pink fluffy dressing gown. Behind her was his dad, wearing his airforce-blue pyjamas. In his arms he was carrying the most special human being in Haatchi's life – his very own Little B.

It was an ordinary Monday morning and all three humans had just woken up, ready to face their day. Owen was off to school as usual, Colleen would soon be heading out to work, and Will would be in and out but mostly at home with him and Mr Pixel.

Before they even put the kettle on or took a shower, though, they all emerged sleepily from their bedrooms and stumbled, yawning, towards where the huge Anatolian Shepherd spent his nights. They opened up the door of the bedroom that kept him safe from further injury and then one by one they crawled inside for a family hug, burying their faces in his soft fur.

Thrilled to see them all, Haatchi licked and snuggled and made joyful gurgling noises as his stump wiggled with excitement. Panting hot doggy breath and groaning with pleasure, the big dog eventually pulled himself up to tower over eight-year-old Owen, the little boy whose life he had transformed.

'Haatchi's smiling!' Owen cried, as he peered up into the furry face of his best buddy. 'Good boy!'

Looking down and squinting through his glasses at the assorted toys on Haatchi's bed, Owen then picked up his favourite and held it out to the gentle giant like an offering. The dog carefully lifted Harold Hedgehog from Owen's tiny cramped hands in jaws powerful enough to snap the neck of a lion. Settling back down onto his bedding, Haatchi held the fluffy toy softly in his mouth, then dropped it and nudged it playfully towards Little B, cocking his head, hopeful for a game.

Colleen and Will curled up together in a comfy corner of the cage and watched happily as Owen took up the challenge and a playful tug-of-war began between a dog and his boy.

Haatchi had been in their lives for only two years, and yet it seemed as if he had always been a part of it.

Both the dog and the boy had a long road ahead of them, but – together – it seemed as if they could take on the world. Rolling around in one giant ball of fur and love, it was almost impossible to see where Haatchi ended and Little B began.

As Will and Colleen wondered if they'd ever get Owen off to school that morning, Haatchi spoke to them in his special doggy talk and their courageous little boy erupted into one of his giggling fits; they could do nothing but throw back their heads and laugh.

**Keep reading
for some puzzles and
extra information!**

Find Haatchi

Can you figure out the right path
to lead you to Haatchi?

START

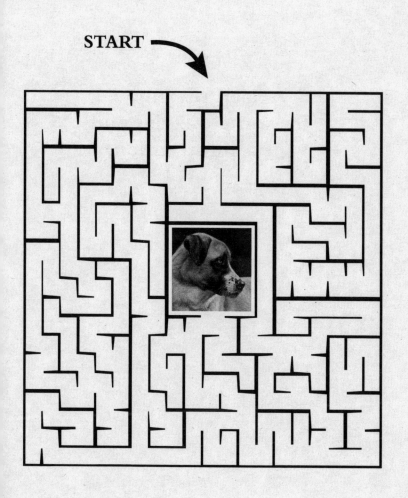

My Dog

Little B and Haatchi are best friends and do everything together. Draw a picture of your dog in the space below.

If you don't have a dog, draw one you would like to have.

Where Haatchi got
his name . . .

In reading Owen and Haatchi's story you will have heard about Hachikō. Like Haatchi he was an incredible dog and a friend to his human. Here is some more about him . . .

Hachikō was a golden-brown Akita dog who lived in the 1920s with his owner, Hidesabur Ueno, a professor at the University of Tokyo in Japan.

Every single day Hachikō would pad over to the train station to meet Professor Ueno when he came back from work so they could walk home together. But one day, disaster struck. The Professor was seriously ill at work and did not return home to the station where Hachikō was waiting as usual.

Hachikō still looked after Professor Ueno's wife, but every day he padded over to the train station to wait for his master. He was always exactly on time for the train the professor used to travel on.

Soon, people at the station and on the trains

started to notice Hachikō still waiting all by himself. They would bring him treats and food while he waited.

This was a long time ago and Hachikō grew old and sadly died, but the place where he waited every day now has some special pawprints and a plaque to explain what an incredible, loyal dog he was

Lots of people and organizations have
helped Haatchi. You can find out more
about these at their websites:

www.rspca.org.uk/home

**www.rspca.org.uk/local/harmsworth-
memorial-animal-hospital/**

www.alldogsmatter.co.uk

If you have enjoyed reading about Haatchi and Owen, you will love these real-life stories about humans and their animal best friends . . .

Meet Norton and Peter as they travel the world together . . .

Peter Gethers hates cats. That is until he meets Norton, a very cute, very friendly Scottish Fold kitten.

Soon Peter and Norton are inseparable, travelling together on trains and boats, in planes and cars all over the world! Eating at restaurants, making new friends and meeting famous movie stars – read all about these and Norton's other real-life adventures in this wonderful true story.

AVAILABLE NOW – ISBN: 978 1 849 41387 9

Meet Jon and the dogs of Bedlam Farm . . .

THE TOTALLY TRUE STORY OF

DEVON

The Naughtiest Dog in the World

Jon Katz

Based on *A Dog Year*, the *Sunday Times* bestseller

DEVON:
THE NAUGHTIEST DOG
IN THE WORLD
ISBN: 978 1 849 41110 3

ROSE & IZZY:
THE CHEEKIEST DOGS
ON THE FARM
ISBN: 978 1 849 41278 0

LENORE:
THE HUNGRIEST DOG IN THE WORLD
ISBN: 978 1 849 41554 5

Meet Ace, John and Christian the lion . . .

It's almost Christmas and as two friends search for gifts
in London they come across the most unbelievable
sight – a lion for sale in the famous store, Harrods!

Unable to bear the thought of leaving the little cub,
Ace and John take him home and name him Christian.
A year of fun and mischief later, Christian has
grown up and Ace and John must find him a new
home back in his native Africa.

AVAILABLE NOW – ISBN: 978 1 862 30956 2